# Autumn
# meditations

## JOHN BARTUNEK, LC, SThD

Liguori

*Imprimi Potest:*
Stephen T. Rehrauer, CSsR, Provincial
Denver Province, the Redemptorists

*Imprimi Potest:*
Fr. John Connor, LC, Territorial Director
Territory of Northern America, Legionaries of Christ

Published by Liguori Publications
Liguori, Missouri 63057

To order, visit Liguori.org or call 800-325-9521.

### Library of Congress Cataloging-in-Publication Data

Names: Bartunek, John, author
Title: Autumn meditations / Fr. John Bartunek, LC, SThD
Description: First Edition. | Liguori: Liguori Publications, 2016
Identifiers: LCCN 2016034366 | ISBN 9780764825637
Subjects: LCSH: Autumn—Religious aspects—Christianity—Meditations.
    Spiritual exercises.
Classification: LCC BV135.A98 B37 2016 | DDC 242—dc23
LC record available at https://lccn.loc.gov/2016034366
e ISBN 978-0-7648-7014-9

Liguori Publications, a nonprofit corporation, is an apostolate of the Redemptorists. To learn more about the Redemptorists, visit Redemptorists.com.

Printed in the United States of America
20 19 18 17 16  /  5 4 3 2 1
First Edition

# Table of Contents

# Introduction

We don't need scientific studies to tell us today's culture is out of touch with nature, even though plenty of such studies are available. Not only are various social pockets engaged in industrial activities that have dangerous effects on the environment, but also few of us post-modern people are able to live our lives in harmony with the natural rhythms of the earth.

In fact, we tend to ignore them, whether consciously or not. We can make daytime seem like nighttime and nighttime seem like daytime. We can make winter feel like summer and summer feel like winter. We can travel from the tropics to the tundra in less than a day, from the mountains to the sea in an afternoon. We can find whatever fruit or vegetable we want in our local grocery store, regardless of whether an item is in or out of season.

Our natural environment mostly has become a kind of add-on to our lives. We feel the pangs of weather changes and the panic of natural disasters—as yet we haven't learned to control such things with technology—but our day-to-day, month-to-month, and year-to-year lives have, in general, gotten out of synch with the natural rhythms of the earth we were created to live in.

This can cause problems. As human beings, our lives are meant to unfold in harmony with the natural world. The seasons, the processes of nature, the rhythms of this world—our world— were created out of love and given to us as a home. They have something to tell us about our deeper identities, the purpose of our lives, the way to live our lives to the full. When we cut ourselves off from direct, regular, and necessary contact with and dependence on this natural environment, we threaten to sever an ancient and irreplaceable link to authentic wisdom. This is why I decided to write these meditations.

## A Needed Return to Natural Wisdom

The bite-sized chapters in these meditation books (this is the third of four) will provide you with some space to remember and reconnect with this essential dimension of your humanity. That, by the way, is what meditation means: giving yourself the time and space, both physically and psychologically, to reflect calmly and deeply on important spiritual values. It is my sincere hope that by doing so you will experience a spiritual and emotional revitalization. You will be able to escape from the ceaseless, inhuman, digitized grind of life and regain balance.

I'm not accusing you of being unspiritual. I'm banking on the fact that even though you have hope, courage, faith, and love, you still feel a hunger to have *more* of them—a deeper faith, a more vibrant hope, a more dynamic courage. That's one of the great things about spiritual values. Because they are spiritual, they can always keep growing.

## Avoiding the Rush

This volume contains twelve meditations, one per week of the season. But at the end of each meditation you will find some suggested activities to help you absorb the nourishing truths the meditation explained (the "Making It Your Own" sections). A good way to make use of this book is to read a meditation at the beginning of the week, underlining, highlighting, and writing in the margins as you reflect on what you read. Then for the rest of the week, take time each day to review your highlights and to put into practice one of the suggested activities. Following that method will assure that whatever good ideas you find as you read will have sufficient time and space to seep from your mind into your heart and your spirit, fostering personal renewal.

## Getting Personal

These meditations contain many personal anecdotes that I think help illustrate my points. I also hope that making myself vulnerable in this way will encourage you to reflect on the richness of your own life experience to find the lessons, the nuggets of wisdom, that God, in his generous providence, always offers to you.

May this volume of simple meditations on the season of fall be a window through which you can discover, once again, the "dearest freshness deep down things"[1] that have always nourished what is best in the human spirit.

[1] From Gerard Manley Hopkins' poem "God's Grandeur"

# Chapter 1: *Trust*

Like spring, autumn is a transitional season. As we enjoy the fruits of summer, we have a chance to look back on those months and evaluate them with the luxury of hindsight. Through that lens, we can see that all those summer storms, challenges, and crises, as real as they were, couldn't hold back the steady maturing and unfolding of the fruits of the earth. The power of life and the guidance of providence, as subtle, mundane, and unobtrusive as they so often seem, are dependable. We can count on them. We can work with them. We can have confidence in them.

This confidence is more easily felt when we can gaze on the fruits of our labors than when we are planting, watering or fertilizing, and there seems to be too much rain or too little, or when the violent tempests of summer are unleashing their full force upon our seemingly small and vulnerable projects. After the drama subsides and the harvest is in, we can easily stir up inner tranquility, the assurance that comes when we anchor ourselves in the bedrock of trust.

Autumn is a teacher of trust. In the springtimes of life we launch out on new adventures, we sow and plant and break ground on new projects. We are moved to do so by hope. We are sometimes disappointed. Things don't always work out precisely as we hoped them to, even if they are still becoming enriching in some way. This is why hope is nourished by trust. We can hope more daringly if we trust in the goodness and power of Providence, in the rhythms and innate fruitfulness of earthly life. This is what autumn teaches us to do. As we carve our pumpkins and peel our apples and gather our wheat, we are shown vividly, once again, that the harvest does come, that the spring planting and the summer tending are worth it. Hope does not, in the end, disappoint.

When I left my job to join the seminary, my dad wasn't happy with my decision. At the time, he thought being a priest was a waste of my education, my talent, and my life—and he said so pretty clearly. He was so vehemently against my pursuit of a priestly vocation that I sincerely thought he might refuse to talk to me again if I went through with it. But off I went anyway.

During my first years of formation, I didn't come back home to visit, and my dad didn't come to the seminary to see me. We corresponded by letter. I tried to describe how engaging the formation process was, how much I was growing spiritually, emotionally, and intellectually. But he didn't buy it. His return letters were not encouraging. On the contrary, he filled them with biting sarcasm and other painful attacks and criticisms. Through it all, I hoped and prayed. I didn't want to lose the friendship I had with my dad, but I felt helpless to do anything about his resistance to my calling. At the time, I wasn't even praying for his conversion. I was just praying that we would somehow be able to stay on speaking terms. I prayed, and I trusted, and I prayed again. It was a long and stormy two calendar years filled with what seemed like blind hopes for a healthy harvest.

When my novitiate was over, I arranged to visit my dad. I was nervous. After the novitiate I was more convinced than ever that God was calling me to the priesthood, and I wanted to follow the call. I didn't know how my father was going to react, and I didn't know how I would react to his reaction.

Then he began to tell me about an encounter he had recently while at work one day. He was walking on the sidewalk when he ran into an old high school buddy whom he hadn't seen in years. The friend asked my dad about his kids. My dad told him that my siblings were doing just fine but didn't mention me. So when his friend asked, "What about John?" My dad answered reluctantly, "John's going to be a Catholic priest."

My dad went into detail about his friend's reaction: "So then he stops walking, he stands there on the sidewalk, and he turns toward me and looks me in the eye. He got this kind of surprised, kind of eager look on his face. And then he says to me, 'Well! At least *someone's* doing something worthwhile with his life!'" That's when my dad turned toward me, looked right at me, smiled, and said, "I guess that's a kind of compliment."

And I smiled right back at him. I knew my prayers had been answered: He had accepted my vocation.

Jesus put it beautifully during his Last Supper. His apostles had put all their hopes in him. They had left everything to follow him, and Jesus knew that a storm was coming. He knew he was going to be betrayed, arrested, unjustly condemned, tortured and humiliated, and eventually crucified. That was the path he would have to travel, a path that could easily extinguish all hope. But he also knew that he was going to rise again from the dead, and he had spoken of this to his followers. Yes, the seed would have to be planted in the furrow and die, but that death would lead to new life, to growth and to multiplication, and to a new harvest:

Amen, amen, I say to you, unless a grain of wheat falls to the ground and dies, it remains just a grain of wheat; but if it dies, it produces much fruit (John 12:24).

This was the pattern his own life, death, and resurrection would set for all his followers. They, too, would have to suffer the summer storms, and their hope would be tested. By learning from the harvest of his resurrection, by learning the lesson of trust that autumn teaches, they would be able to persevere through their trials and come to the joy of their own harvests:

I have told you this so that you might have peace in me. In the world you will have trouble, but take courage, I have conquered the world (John 16:33).

There is room for trust in this world. The storms and the tempests will not have the last word. Providence wins in the end. If we sow well, we will reap well, when the time comes. This, too, we can learn from autumn.

## Making It Your Own

† Choose one sentence from this chapter that really resonated in your heart or compose a one-sentence summary. Write it on a sticky note. Put it where you will see it throughout the week as a reminder that trust nourishes hope, and that autumn teaches us to trust.

† Write down all your hopes on small pieces of paper. Place those pieces of paper in an envelope. Go to a nearby church. Place that envelope on the altar and kneel down in prayer. Offer all your hopes to God, placing them under the protection of his wise and powerful providence. Don't rush; sit there a while, enjoying God's presence as you surrender all your hopes to him. When you're finished, take the envelope back home and put it in a secret box. In a year, open it up and read the hopes. See how God took care of your hopes. Then repeat, but this time when you go to the church, take time to thank him for whatever blessings he sent you during the previous year.

† Take time this week to go for a walk in the woods. Try to find some big oak trees. Look near them for some acorns. Pick up an acorn and examine it. Then examine the full-grown

oak tree. Touch it, admire it, feel its strength and solidity, its massiveness. Compare the two. Every oak tree comes from an acorn. That little acorn has the power within it to become an oak tree. This is life as God has designed it. Discover the lesson of trust in the relationship between the acorn and the oak tree.

† Take time this week to read Psalm 1. It uses plant imagery to describe the difference between someone who trusts in and obeys God and someone who rejects God and his ways. Read the psalm slowly and prayerfully. Notice what strikes you, what desires or memories it stirs up. Write them down in a journal. What is God teaching you through this psalm?

† Take time this week to prayerfully reflect on some disappointments you have had in your life. Go back over them to see what lessons they taught you. In conversation with God, try to come to terms with them. Allow trust in God's wisdom and power to heal any leftover resentment or discouragement. "In the world you will have trouble; but take courage, I have conquered the world" (John 16:33).

# **Chapter 2:** *Joy*

The joy of autumn is the joy of the harvest. The long hours of sweating in the summer heat yield to crisp fall air and the gathering of fruits. Grapes heavy on the vine, bunches of apples weighing down their branches, noble stalks of wheat shining golden in the autumn light, all eager to be gathered in. The vegetable gardens show off their prizes, pumpkins and squash and gourds of strange and wonderful shapes; watermelons and cantaloupes and zucchini plump and luscious after drinking in the summer sun; tomatoes and peppers and cucumbers by the dozen eager to burst open their flavors if you snatch them up before the first frost.

We are all familiar with these images. At least we're familiar with seeing these items on the shelves of our grocery stores. But seeing them on the farm or in the garden is different, especially if you've been watching them since they were planted. The transformation of an almost shapeless seed into a jubilant pumpkin takes time and patience. The sweet crispness of a ripe apple seems to be a world away from the sweet softness of the airy apple blossoms that sung forth their bewitching scent in the spring—a truly marvelous transformation.

The joy of the harvest is multidimensional for those who pause to reflect. The first dimension is simply the abundance of good produce that nourishes us and keeps our economy flowing. The delightful colors, smells, and tastes of the mature fruits create a second dimension of joy, of enjoyment. The mysterious, awe-inspiring drama behind the harvest—the very process of planting, growing, and maturing—opens up a third dimension, that of *spiritual* joy, which can feed our souls if we let it.

Our lives are like those plants. Many spiritual writers have likened the human soul to a garden, where God plants seeds of spiritual fruit that must be watered, tended, nourished, and patiently cared for to come to fruition. These seeds can be ideas. They can be experiences that jar us or that we barely recognize at all in the moment. But these seeds put down roots in the soil of our memory and then grow and flower, filling us with new insights and understandings that enrich who we are and how we interact with others.

When I was a novice learning the ropes of religious life, I had all kinds of problems. The ascetical demands of following a monastic schedule and accepting the limitations of a vow of poverty grated on the habits of ease and comfort that I had formed during my college and post-collegiate years. The conflicts of living in a community of people chosen by God and not by my own preference brought daily trials and frustrations. Learning to follow the religious rule of life in spite of violent mood swings and irrational feelings of rebellion revealed to me just how spiritually immature I was and how much purification I needed if I were to become a useful priest.

The difficulties continued throughout my years of formation. The daily grind of religious life, without the pleasant distractions I had come to depend on before joining, was a demanding road. It was a long summer full of backbreaking work and spiritual sweat under the hot sun of my own egoism and concupiscence.

But then I got a glimpse of the harvest. I was sent to a remote, poor town in Mexico. I arrived on Palm Sunday and met the group of families from Mexico City who were going to spend Holy Week on a spiritual and humanitarian mission there. They planned to visit every local family, organize activities for the children, formation and instruction for the adults, and finally invite everyone to come and participate in the glorious Holy Week liturgies. I was there for those liturgies, to anoint the sick and dying, and to hear confessions.

All day every day, when I wasn't celebrating the liturgy, preaching, or visiting the sick, I was hearing confessions. The town had no full-time priest of its own, so this was the only time the sacrament was available.

It was my first year of priesthood, and it was the first time I sat down to hear confessions in that way. I was nervous. But as soon as the first penitent arrived, I began to glimpse the harvest.

The difficulties God had permitted me to face and grow through during my seminary formation had not been in vain. The lessons enabled me to empathize with the more dramatic sufferings of the people I was ministering to, and the comfort and guidance God had given me turned out to be comfort and guidance that was equally valid, equally useful and encouraging, for them.

Those hours and hours of confessions became hours and hours of joy, the joy of the harvest, the joy of seeing the fruits of a marvelous process of spiritual planting, growing, and maturing.

The Book of Psalms depicts the joy of the harvest with a striking image:

> You adorn the year with your bounty;
> your paths drip with fruitful rain.
>
> The meadows of the wilderness also drip;
> the hills are robed with joy.
>
> The pastures are clothed with flocks,
> the valleys blanketed with grain;
> they cheer and sing for joy.

*Psalm 65:12–14*

Let's not miss the joy of the harvest. Let's not miss its many levels. Let's join the celebration by taking the time to marvel at how the strong, gentle hand of Providence turns blossoms into apples, shapeless seeds into raucous, pudgy pumpkins, and jarring experiences into spiritual fruits.

The joy of the harvest, whether material or spiritual, is a joy that only comes to those who wait, to those who persevere in their duties and patiently allow the wonderful mysteries of life on this earth to unfold as God intends them to.

## Making It Your Own

&#8224; Choose one sentence from this chapter that really resonated in your heart or compose a one-sentence summary. Write it on a sticky note. Put it where you will see it throughout the week as a reminder that the joy of the harvest is meant to be part of the rhythm of life.

&#8224; Take time this week to go to a farm, a greenhouse, or a garden. Give yourself permission to gaze with wonder at the amazing process. Let this experience bring you back in touch with the rhythms of God's awe-inspiring creation.

&#8224; Prayerfully reflect on the spiritual garden that is your soul. Write in a journal the different spiritual plants that are growing there. Maybe you'll find fruitful ones like patience, faith, wisdom, or weeds like resentment, frustration, discouragement. Ask God to show you how you can root out the bad and cultivate the good.

&#8224; Eat some of your favorite autumn foods this week. Enjoy them, savor them. As you do, feel God enjoying them with you. The good things of the earth are his gift to us, and when we enjoy them properly we give him pleasure.

† This week, take your Bible into a quiet corner or onto a park bench, somewhere with a nice view of nature, and read prayerfully Psalms 65 and 104. Both speak to us about God's presence in his creation. As you read, pause when a verse or a phrase resonates with you. Let it linger as long as it wishes to before moving on. Use this experience to find God's presence in his creation, and then ask for the grace to do so more and more easily as you continue your journey of life.

# Chapter 3: *Acceptance*

Summer doesn't last forever. Gradually, the days begin to shorten again. The warm breeze becomes cooler. Carefree children button back up for another year of school. This is the way of things here on earth. They come and go, just like the seasons. We need to learn to accept that rhythm, not resist it.

Acceptance based on a humility that faces and embraces the simple truth of reality is a life-giving virtue. Here, autumn's signature characteristic encourages us. When the light dims and the temperature drops, the trees sense that summer is over. They begin to release their leaves to prepare for the coming winter. The green leaves have done their job of producing food for the tree, and so the chlorophyll breaks down, surrendering its dominant green color to other pigments present in the leaves. Thus emerges the splendor of autumn, the silent symphony of yellow-, gold-, red-, bronze-, purple-, and maroon-colored leaves that flash out in their brilliance just long enough to say goodbye to summer and hello to winter.

There is glory in their surrender. There can be glory, too, in our surrender, in our humble, interior acceptance of change that comes whether we want it to or not, whether we feel ready for it or afraid of it. There is beauty in accepting our limitations. Sometimes, in fact, only in accepting them do we actually discover the beauty—the splendorous colors beneath the green—hidden within us.

About six years before my father died, he had heart surgery. The doctors had to repair a valve, and at the same time they installed a quadruple bypass. Fortunately, he had been conscientious about exercise and diet, so he was able to make a satisfactory recovery. Even so, he wasn't as strong as he had been, and because he was living alone, I was concerned. He couldn't maintain the same level of activity that he had previously enjoyed, so I knew that loneliness might soon make its appearance. And in spite of his successful recovery, the surgery had taken a toll on him. To me it looked as if he had aged ten years in ten months.

Circumstances made it possible for me to start visiting him more frequently than before. I thought I knew what this providence meant: It was time for my dad to start believing in God again and come back to the Church. By this time I was a priest with some experience, so I was sure that God was giving me this new opportunity so I could convert my dad.

My initial efforts yielded pitiful results. Whenever I brought up topics related to the faith or the spiritual life, my dad would shut down. I don't think it was a conscious resistance. Rather, it was just that he didn't think in those terms. So I enlisted some help. I asked some good Catholics I knew to pay him a visit. Other friends did so even without my nudging. But still, no sign of progress.

I tried harder. I brought him books. I left rosaries lying around the house. I prayed for him harder and more frequently. I signed him up to receive Catholic publications. I used all the creativity I could muster in order to come up with new ways to get him interested in the faith. Nothing worked.

Finally, frustrated and exhausted, I brought my concern to the Lord. "What else can I do, Lord? I've tried everything. What's wrong?" God's answer came pretty clearly: "Let it go. Just love him and accompany him." That's what came into my heart, and it had the gentleness and peaceful assurance that comes with true inspirations of the Holy Spirit. So that's what I did. Soon afterward, the glories of autumn began to shine.

During those last years of my dad's life, when I was simply loving and accompanying him, we spent more time together than ever before. We were both free to get to know each other afresh and to enjoy one another in ways that neither one of us had ever imagined could happen. My frequent visits became little whiffs of heaven. That last season of his life really was just like the intense splendor of autumn foliage: surprising, brilliant, inspiring, even breathtaking. And it was a gift that we were able to enjoy only through acceptance.

Even for Jesus, the glory of the resurrection emerged only through his acceptance of the cross. Saint Luke records his last words before dying as a simple but deep prayer of acceptance and surrender: "Jesus cried out in a loud voice, 'Father, into your hands I commend my spirit'; and when he had said this he breathed his last" (Luke 23:46). That's a very good prayer. Let's ask Christ for the grace to learn how to pray it and for the wisdom to know when we need to.

Some things we are meant to fight for or to fight against. But many times we are called to accept these things that seem to be at odds with how we want them to be or think they should be. Only then can the hidden beauty emerge and the new glory shine forth.

## Making It Your Own

&#8224;  Choose one sentence from this chapter that really resonated in your heart or compose a one-sentence summary. Write it on a sticky note. Put it where you will see it throughout the week as a reminder that acceptance can be the secret to releasing hidden glory.

&#8224;  Spend time this week reflecting prayerfully about things that you may need to accept but haven't yet been able to. Think about what may be holding you back. Write down these reflections to help bring your own thoughts and feelings into focus.

&#8224;  Make a list of all the changes that are happening in your life right now: physical and physiological changes, relationship changes, spiritual changes, or simple, practical changes. Go through each one and decide the best way to accept it and live it fruitfully.

&#8224;  Make a list of all the things you would like to change in your life right now but that aren't changing. Then go through that list, deciding prayerfully what you may need to accept and what you may need to do something about. Draw some specific resolutions from this exercise.

† Take time this week to go for a walk in the woods. Don't listen to anything. Turn your phone off. Be alone with the Lord in the midst of his creation. See and hear the rhythms and indications of change that God has built into nature. Discover their beauty and what they mean for you in the here and now of your life.

# Chapter 4: *Faithfulness*

Most people have favorite places: their favorite room in the house or their favorite vacation spot. Most of us also have our favorite outdoor spots: a favorite tree, a favorite garden, a favorite place to go for a walk, a favorite place to have a cookout. In the transitional season of autumn, we can see with particular clarity the qualities that go into making these places so special to us. One of those qualities, without a doubt, is faithfulness.

A favorite tree can only become a favorite tree if it stays rooted, weathering the storms of every season. In autumn, when we become keenly aware of the passing nature of things, we find comfort in going back to that favorite tree, sitting beneath it perhaps, or simply pressing our hands to its sturdy trunk and feeling its rough (or smooth) bark close to our skin. In the midst of everything that changes and passes, we can count on our favorite tree to always be there. It's a symbol of continuity and stability, and as such it allows us to temper the melancholy that inevitably accompanies autumn loss with the deeper, spiritual assurance that the most important things will always, in some mysterious way, endure.

The same goes for a favorite bench in the park. It affords us a view, perhaps, of the river or the fields, the forest or the flowers. Though the details of that view alter while the seasons unfold, as autumn makes abundantly clear, the underlying shape of that particular window onto the world stays the same. Its geography, and its geometry, are faithful and dependable. It is that underlying faithfulness that permits us to enjoy the bittersweet pleasure of watching how its surface features continually transform.

Faithfulness is that underlying dependability that we look for in our relationships. Life flows on without halting. Circumstances continually shift and alter, closing down certain challenges and opportunities while opening up others. As the ancient Greek philosopher Heraclitus put it, you can never step into the same river twice, because the river's water never stops flowing and changing. And yet, in the midst of the ineluctable reality of constant change, we need anchors. We need relationships built on solider stuff, like mutual knowledge and understanding, love and affection, respect and shared experience. Those are spiritual values that escape the flow of life's river, or rather they are the riverbed that gives the ever-flowing water its shape and direction, its meaning.

They whisper to our souls an echo of God's own promise of eternal life, of a life so full that it transcends all possibility of loss and sadness:

> I have loved you with an everlasting love…
> He will wipe every tear from their eyes, and
> there shall be no more death or mourning,
> wailing or pain, [for] the old order has
> passed away.
>
> *Jeremiah 31:3,* English Standard Version;
> *Revelation 21:4*

It happened on Christmas afternoon in 2003, in Rome. I had been ordained to the priesthood the day before, and concelebrated Christmas Eve midnight Mass in the same chapel where I had been ordained. But on Christmas I took off with my older sister and several family friends to celebrate my first solo Mass.

For this solemn occasion I had chosen a side altar in the chapel of the crucifix in the Church of Santa Maria del Popolo. Martin Luther had used that same altar for Mass during a trip to Rome, when he was still a Catholic priest and monk. My faith journey had begun in a Protestant church, and my heart was full of desires for renewed unity among all Christians. I wanted to celebrate my first Mass there as a way to thank God for my own conversion, to make reparation for sins of division in the body of Christ, and to beg God for Christian unity.

Even though I had practiced plenty, I was still nervous when I processed out to the altar. The Mass is the perfect prayer. In the Mass, through the Eucharist, Jesus himself is present in a unique way, mysteriously collapsing history and distance to bring every here and now into his redeeming presence on the cross at Calvary.

The sacredness of the Mass is preserved and protected by the priest's duty to follow the established ritual, and as I prayed those words over the bread and the wine, allowing the Holy Spirit to transform them into Christ's Body and Blood, I began to weep. The bread, the wine, that day and time, my very self, were all such fragile and impermanent things, and yet, those very things were being swept up by God's providence into the realm of the everlasting. They were becoming instruments of and partners with the divine. At one and the same time, I was engaged in an action that was more significant than any I had ever done before or would ever do again, and yet I myself was just a servant. Time and eternity came together on that altar in such a way that I felt what seemed like an impossibly joyful agony in which my passing and temporal being was pierced through with the dynamic permanence of eternity.

So faithful was God that he allowed me to plug my small and time-bound life into the very source of unchanging, everlasting grace.

Here again the Psalms speak eloquently of the human predicament. We are subject to the sad impermanence of all earthly things, and yet beyond the aches of loss and decay a divine goodness dwells, calling out with a voice that only the very center of our hearts can hear to give us the cheerful assurance that as long as we live in friendship with God (expressed in Old Testament terms by "the fear of the Lord"), his faithfulness and love—his unending mercy—will restore all losses and lead us to the life that never fades.

> As for man, his days are like the grass;
> he blossoms like a flower in the field.
>
> A wind sweeps over it and it is gone;
> its place knows it no more.
>
> But the LORD's mercy is from age to age,
> toward those who fear him.
>
> *Psalm 103:15–17*

Life on earth includes a constant tension between what endures and what passes, a tension that gives our human experience much of its peculiar pathos and wondrous creativity. We carry in our souls a spark of eternity: "...He, meanwhile, has made the world, in all its seasonable beauty, and has set eternity in their hearts..." (Ecclesiastes 3:11, *Knox* translation).

As we make our way through this earthly pilgrimage to our everlasting home, then, faithfulness, like the dependability found in our favorite places, gives our swirling lives a firm anchor and solid foundation. It is, in a sense, the face of eternity, perhaps even the face of God himself. It looks at us with a smile whenever we look toward it, stirring up the strength we need to continue forward, to gather the fruits of summer, and to prepare for the scarcity of winter, without despairing of the value of our efforts.

## Making It Your Own

† Choose one sentence from this chapter that really resonated in your heart or compose a one-sentence summary. Write it on a sticky note. Put it where you will see it throughout the week as a reminder that faithfulness gives shape and meaning to all things that pass away.

† Take time this week to go to one of your favorite places and simply gaze at it. Contemplate its features, those that change and those that underlie and permit the change. Pay attention to the thoughts and desires that arise in your heart as you engage in that contemplation. Write them down in your journal as a way of bringing them into focus.

† Reach out this week to one of your friends, family members, or acquaintances who is dealing with a painful loss. Invite the person out for lunch or over for a cup of tea. Use the encounter to remind the individual, with words or without, that although material things pass away, spiritual things endure. "God is faithful" (1 Corinthians 1:19).

† Think of someone in your life who has given you the experience of faithfulness, someone who has been faithful in spite of life's changing uncertainties. Thank God for that person, then reach out and thank that person.

† Take time this week to prayerfully review how you are living the quality of faithfulness. Reflect on the key relationships and duties in your life and evaluate the degree of faithfulness you are showing in each of them. Celebrate the good things that you discover through this exercise, and make a specific resolution about how you can improve your faithfulness in at least one area of your life. Write it in your calendar to help you remember it.

# Chapter 5: *Elegance*

During the summer, when all the trees reach out to the heavens with their branches sumptuously adorned by a joyous abundance of green leaves, you can't always see the unique shape of each individual tree. The common green color makes the trees blend into each other. It gives the general impression of exuberance and vitality, without highlighting the unique form of any individual arbor.

That changes in the autumn. When the leaves begin to stand out because of their colors, each tree takes on its own particular hue. And so, for those weeks when the green is gone but before the leaves have fallen, the individual shape of each tree becomes much easier to discern. You feel, as if you are meeting each tree anew, getting to know it in a deeper way, when you discover its distinctive form. In those conditions, this created world reveals afresh its natural elegance, its poise and composure, its harmonious blend of inimitable individuality and shared complementarity.

When you climb a hill or a mountainside at this time of year, you can sit on a rock and gaze down at a valley decked with a Tuscan palette of colors and overflowing with an equally diverse variation of shapes. They all look like trees. They all share enough characteristics that you can agree about their "tree-ness." But when you gaze long enough you see that the shape of the maple is not the shape of the oak, and the form of the poplar has little to do with that of the chestnut. And even between two maples, even when they are the same kind of maple, subtle differences give each one its inimitable, breathtaking beauty. Only autumn affords us the chance to feast our eyes on this display, this silent and motionless dance of elegant array.

The most elegant corner of the world, in my experience, is Pazzi Chapel, a small structure built as an addendum to the magnificent Italian Gothic church of Santa Croce, in Florence, Italy. Pazzi Chapel was conceived and designed by Filippo Brunelleschi, the fourteenth-century Florentine genius who had such a disproportionately large share in launching the Italian Renaissance.

Before I had thoroughly studied the theory behind Renaissance architecture, I had the grace to experience its reality simply by wandering into places like this chapel. The way it is designed, constructed, and decorated creates a space that literally changes your mood when you walk into it. The shapes used in construction and decoration are simple: squares, rectangles, and circles, all related to each other through calculated geometric precision and harmonious three-dimensional intersection. The visual rhythms of those shapes and proportions are reiterated by the purity of the colors.

Entering Pazzi Chapel is like entering another realm. The chapel immediately communicates order, serenity, and calm. But not the dead calm of emptiness. Rather, the productive and inspiring calm and order of purposeful vitality.

Nothing extraneous distracts the mind or the heart; nothing escapes the integral harmony by trying to stand on its own; nothing betrays the dynamic unity that makes of this space a living, breathing invitation to elevate the soul and cleanse it of all pettiness, confusion, and angst. It is pure elegance.

The person who introduced me to this place was one of the first truly elegant people whom I had ever met: Maria Fossi Todorow. She was our art history professor during the time I was studying in Florence. A descendant of Florentine aristocracy, an accomplished scholar and museum curator, a brilliant professor, and a woman of deep and sincere faith, she turned out to be a true messenger from the Lord for me.

As she taught us about the great achievements of the Renaissance, I found myself falling in love with all that artistic beauty. But I wanted to learn more. I began to see that it was all connected to the Catholic faith—the paintings, the sculptures, the architectural spaces—they all expressed not just an aesthetic point of view, but a religious sensibility. My desire to penetrate the secrets of this overwhelming beauty moved me to ask the professor if she could start teaching us more about the religious inspiration behind these artistic marvels. She demurred. It wasn't a Catholic university, after all. She must have seen some disappointment in my eyes, because she asked, "But, do you really want to learn about the Catholic faith?" I answered with an eager and determined "yes."

She took it upon herself to guide me along a parallel track of instruction, sending me on small quests to little-known cultural sites and introducing me to wise spiritual mavens, each of whom patiently fielded my impertinent questions and commented on my naïve observations. As a result, I not only fell in love with Renaissance art that year, but I also fell in love with the Church, and that was the beginning of my priestly vocation.

Maria was elegant not only in her manners and personal presentation but in the highly sensitive and simple restraint with which she encouraged my search for greater understanding. She pointed things out, made suggestions, and arranged situations but left it up to me to take the next step. She advised and encouraged, and she responded generously when I sought guidance and assistance. Like the works of art she introduced us to, her very presence was a gentle but constant invitation to leave behind all pettiness, extravagance, and superfluity and focus on what really mattered.

Elegance, in this sense, goes beyond material things like clothes and furniture. It also infuses the very behavior of anyone who dares to live with the joyful humility that comes from accepting God's unconditional love. That happiness in being oneself, without the need for extraneous frills, nourishes a countenance and a wisdom that in turn bring delight and inspiration to others. The elegance of an autumn panorama thus speaks to us of the elegance of God's grace, which sculpts our very lives into works of art:

> For by grace you have been saved through faith, and this is not from you; it is the gift of God...For we are his handiwork, created in Christ Jesus for the good works that God has prepared in advance, that we should live in them (Ephesians 2:8, 10).

Most dictionaries define elegance with modifiers like "gracefulness" and "dignity." But the type of beauty that qualifies as elegant is always associated, in some way or another, with a certain restraint or simplicity. We see this at work in the beauty of the fall foliage. Each tree is full and abundant in itself, and yet it cedes to those around it. None seems to exhaust, or even to try to exhaust, every possibility of shape and color. Rather, each one presents itself intensely and joyfully, but demurely, within the limits of its reach, happy to be where it is and what it is, without seeming to compete or expand beyond its natural confines. This effortless restraint and winsome simplicity—this elegance—assures that the autumn landscape is always inviting and never intimidating.

## Making It Your Own

† Choose one sentence from this chapter that really resonated in your heart or compose a one-sentence summary. Write it on a sticky note. Put it where you will see it throughout the week as a reminder of the power and beauty released by the graceful and simple restraint of elegance.

† Reflect prayerfully this week on your daily life or on your typical week. To what extent do they show balance, order, and proportion? To what extent are they chaotic and frazzled? Try to identify some concrete aspects that you can adjust to begin enjoying more thoroughly the space in which your life unfolds.

† Jesus advised his followers to "seek first the kingdom of God and his righteousness, and all these things will be given you besides" (Matthew 6:33). He wants us to put our relationship with him at the center of our lives, and build everything else around that. What would you say is at the center of your life right now? What would an objective observer say is at the center of your life? Write down in a journal the thoughts and feelings that come to you as you make this reflection to bring them into focus better.

† Take time this week to visit one of the more renowned architectural sites near where you live. Perhaps take a friend with you. Maybe it is an old church downtown, or your city's art museum, or the symphony hall. Learn about the architectural style before going, then allow yourself to experience how the shaped space communicates itself to you when you are in it, the moods and feelings that it stirs up, the resonances that it strikes in your soul. Use this experience to increase your sensitivity to all the spaces in which your life unfolds.

† Write in a journal unrushed descriptions of the three most beautiful things you have ever seen. Describe them in detail, highlighting what in your mind most contributes to their beauty. Write down the feelings that they inspire in you. Then reflect prayerfully on the feelings you would like to be able to inspire in others and how you might be able to go about doing so in the coming week.

# Chapter 6: *Gratitude*

In North America, one of the great autumn holidays is Thanksgiving. Both Canada and the United States reserve a day during the harvest season to give thanks to the Lord for the blessings he showers upon us. Through the years, this spirit of thanksgiving has overflowed to include gratitude toward other people as well.

The holiday affords us, both as individuals and as a society, a chance to turn our attention away from the self-focused worries that tend to dominate our consciousness. Instead, we spend a day thinking about the rest of the world and how many good things we have received through the goodness of God's providence and the generosity of those who care for us. Gratitude opens our hearts and minds, refreshing them both and curing, or at least giving us a respite from, egoism.

Autumn is the perfect season for such a holiday. The abundance of the harvest always stirs up amazement and rejoicing. As hard as we work during the summer, the fruits of the earth and of our labors always seem a bit more impressive than our own work could make them. We do our part tending the gardens and keeping the fields, but the forces of nature beyond our reach, the inextinguishable impulse toward growth and fruitfulness, yield results far surpassing our stark human powers.

Even our achievements in less agricultural areas—like business, art, or politics—flow from many different sources. The most successful businessman and the most brilliant politician usually rise to their positions not only on the tide of personal talent but also through many influences beyond their control: an attentive teacher, a generous mentor, a happy coincidence, a serendipitous opportunity, a lesson learned in an unplanned circumstance. The self-made man is a myth. Even those who strive most for success only achieve it with the aid of others. They, too, must give thanks for all that they are, all that they have, and all that they have been able to accomplish.

This is why the images of thanksgiving spark joy as well as humility: the cornucopia overflowing with fruits of the earth, the fallen leaves with their glorious but fading colors, the community of extended family and friends gathered around a feast-filled table. All that we have and enjoy comes from a combination of our own smarts and strengths and a whole network of people and factors far beyond our control.

I wrote in a previous season's meditations about the Serbian countess, a 105-year-old widow with whom I boarded during a summer I spent in Venice. I wrote of how she taught me about interior beauty and the power of authentic love, but she also taught me about the power of gratitude.

At the end of my stay with her we were both sad. As we spent more time together and got to know each other, and as her wisdom and goodness helped guide me through a treacherous period in my journey, a true friendship had sprung up. Neither one of us really wanted to see that season come to an end. And yet, it had to.

As my departure day drew near, I found myself desiring to express my immeasurable gratitude to this remarkable lady who had so providentially entered into the unfolding story of my life. I didn't know how to do so. So I continued to reflect and pray until an idea came to me.

It occurred to me that I could give her a music box. I could find one that was elegant and lovely, that wouldn't look out of place among the other decorative items in her palazzo. This would be the perfect gift, the perfect expression of what she had been for me during those months: a beautiful spiritual song that was hidden beneath a worn and overlooked exterior.

Of course, I couldn't have explained that to her face to face. It would have been too emotional, the kind of encounter I tended to avoid at that stage of my life. But I could write it in a letter, and I could leave the letter and the music box on the dresser in my room. Surely she would find it after I left, and she would then discover how grateful I was to her.

That's what I did. I left the letter and the gift on my dresser, and we said goodbye gently and sadly.

She was still my legal host, however, so I had left her information about where I would be staying as I made my way out of the country. The very next day I received a call from her! She had found the letter and the music box, and she wanted to call me to thank me. We only spoke briefly but what she told me has stayed with me even after all these years. She said she had never received such a beautiful gift, that she didn't feel she deserved it, but it made her very happy.

I was so glad that she called. It filled me with joy to know she had understood what I wanted the gift to say and that she cared enough to track me down to tell me so. The sadness that had marked our parting dissipated with that phone call. I had thanked her, and she had thanked me, and nothing remained unsaid. That phone conversation was the last time we spoke. She died before I was able to return to Venice. But even death couldn't take away the life-giving beauty of our friendship: Our last exchange of mutual gratitude had emblazoned it forever on my heart.

No one understood the importance of gratitude more than Jesus. The Gospels often show him giving thanks to his Father, before the miracle of the multiplication of the loaves, for example, after his disciples came back from their first mission, during the Last Supper. He himself was moved to praise the virtue of gratitude when only one of the ten lepers he cleansed returned to give him thanks, even while he felt the pain of the other nine's ingratitude: "Ten were cleansed, were they not? Where are the other nine? Has none but this foreigner returned to give thanks to God?" (Luke 17:17–18). Jesus knows that an ungrateful heart is a closed heart, and a closed heart cannot receive the love and grace that give meaning to our lives.

Saint Paul, too, makes the connection between humility and gratitude. He wrote to the Christians in Corinth: "What do you possess that you have not received? But if you have received it, why are you boasting as if you did not receive it?" (1 Corinthians 4:7).

In the Catholic tradition, the Mass, our central act of worship and the most perfect prayer, is called the celebration of the Eucharist. The bread and wine that are mysteriously transformed into the Body and Blood of Christ are called "the Eucharist." It's an interesting word. It comes from a Greek root that means, precisely, "Thanksgiving." The highest act of worship and the purest prayer, then, is that of gratitude. Here is what some spiritual writers have called the shortcut to holiness, and holiness is merely another name for true, lasting happiness. As the Letter to the Hebrews puts it: "What gives true strength to a man's heart is gratitude" (Hebrews 13:9, *Knox* translation).

Why not test out whether gratitude really is the shortcut to holiness? Why not see how much strength it gives to the human heart? Why not live the spirit of Thanksgiving every day, instead of only once a year, just to see what happens? I guarantee you won't be disappointed.

## Making It Your Own

† Choose one sentence from this chapter that really resonated in your heart or compose a one-sentence summary. Write it on a sticky note. Put it where you will see it throughout the week as a reminder of the power and importance of gratitude.

† Make a list of all the people who have had a positive influence on your life. Take plenty of time. Write down all their names, no matter how small or seemingly insignificant their influence may have been. Then go back over the list to see how many of those people you have properly thanked. Choose one you haven't yet thanked fully and make a point of doing so this week. Write it in your calendar to help you remember it.

† Reflect prayerfully on your most satisfying accomplishments in life so far. Try to identify your contributions to those accomplishments, and also the contributions of others, either indirectly (through helping you develop the talents that went into them, for example) or directly. Then rejoice in those achievements by offering a prayer of thanksgiving to God for them, glad of the contributions you have made and also of the contributions of others.

† Go to weekday Mass this week. Pay special attention to the words of the prayers throughout the Mass. Notice how the spirit of gratitude is present throughout. Offer this Mass to God in gratitude for some specific blessing you have received from him. Form the habit of thanking God intentionally every time you go to Mass.

† Get together with a family member or two and compose your own prayer before meals, to be used next Thanksgiving and at other family gatherings. Include in it a grateful recognition of God's goodness and the generosity of his providence. Keep it in a special place and read it over at least once a week.

# Chapter 7: *Sadness*

Even amidst the joys of the harvest, autumn always inspires a twinge of sadness. The glories of the autumn landscape are so short-lived. Soon the brilliant leaves lose their luster and fall to the ground. The lovely puddles of color they form under the trees are shortly scattered by the frosty winds. The produce has to be gathered and stored before the harsh winter comes. The stalks and vines, after offering up their fruits, dry out and wither away, mere shadows of their former selves. As a season of transition, fall heralds a new beginning but also harbingers an end. The smiles of autumn tend to be a bit reserved. They are not, like the smiles of spring, looking forward eagerly to a bright and glorious summer but looking back on one. Yes, sadness is part of autumn. Maybe not the largest part, but a hanger-on who cannot be ignored.

Sadness is an emotion all people feel. It is a part of our human nature, part of the fabric of human life. Therefore, it should not simply be ignored or repressed. It must have something to teach us, some valuable lesson that we could never learn otherwise.

There are two kinds of sadness: simple, healthy sadness, and unhealthy discouragement. Since feeling sadness is a basic part of being human, nothing is intrinsically wrong with it. But when we let the feeling of sadness seep into our hearts and minds and extinguish our hope, sadness becomes a danger, a temptation, a threat to the health of our souls. That's discouragement.

An old saying among spiritual writers claims that discouragement never comes from the Holy Spirit. The emotion of sadness can be in harmony with the Holy Spirit's work in our souls, but that kind of sadness is different from discouragement. Since sadness comes simply from recognizing the brokenness of a fallen world, it doesn't paralyze us and extinguish our hope. That kind of sadness strengthens our hearts against evil and actually feeds our courage.

Discouragement, on the other hand, is sadness gone wild. Like a wound that has become infected, discouragement is sadness that starts to fester, and it produces spiritual poison. To become discouraged means to lose the energy necessary to continue forward. To become discouraged is to play with the temptation to give up and give in, to stop trying.

Someone who is discouraged no longer strives after the worthy goal that he used to believe in, because he no longer has any hope that the goal is attainable. And that is why discouragement can never come from the Holy Spirit. In Christ, with the help of God's grace, every worthy goal is always attainable either in this world or the next. That's why discouragement always hides a lie, whereas simple sadness is linked to truth.

Once when I was on Holy Week missions in a poor village in Mexico, one of my fellow missionaries came up to me to say that an old man in the town didn't want to come to the church for confession, but his wife wanted the priest to come to him. As soon as I had a free moment, we set out to see him.

His tiny house, little more than a shack, was located on the outskirts of town. His wife welcomed us with a sincere smile and gracious bow and invited us into the back yard, where her husband was sitting.

As we made our way to the back yard and sat down near the old man, I was wondering what this could be about. I had brought the holy oils, thinking that perhaps the man was too sick to come to town and wanted to receive the sacraments, but he didn't look ill.

We chatted briefly for a minute or two. It didn't take long for the man to bring up what was on his mind. It had to do with his daughter. Some years earlier she had disobeyed him in a grave matter and abandoned the family. Recently, she had returned home to apologize. But when she confronted her father, he was unable to accept her back under his roof. She went away grief-stricken and hopeless. The ongoing estrangement was a torture for the rest of the family.

As he described the tragedy, I could see the anguish on his wife's face and the pain on his own. I started to ask him some questions to understand the situation more fully. The other missionary and I kept trying to convince him that his daughter was truly sorry for her sin, which he viewed as a dishonor to the whole family, and that he should forgive her and accept her back home. He kept insisting that he could not do so. At first, he spoke with pride and strength. But as the conversation progressed, his tone began to change. He couldn't bring himself to forgive his daughter, because he simply didn't know how. He wanted to be able to do so, but he couldn't. His decision had to stand. He couldn't go back on it.

Clearly he was being torn apart by the situation. I was sure that if we simply continued talking, he would find the strength to move forward and reconcile with his daughter. But I was wrong. He wouldn't do it. He wouldn't try. Nothing I said would make him budge, and he wouldn't come to confession because he knew that to do so he would have to forgive her, a possibility he refused.

I offered a prayer for him and the family, and then we left.

The walk back to the church was one of the longest I can remember. My heart was broken. This man was so close to reconciling with his daughter. He knew it was the right thing to do. Part of him, it seemed, wanted to do it. And yet something was holding him back. Something in him was so broken that reconciliation remained outside his grasp.

As I walked I prayed, and a battle started to rage in my own heart. Why couldn't I help this man? Why couldn't God's grace reach him? What had I done wrong? I could feel the icy fingers of discouragement trying to grip my soul. What kind of a priest was I to let this happen? What right did I have to preach about God's mercy and grace if I couldn't communicate it to those who most needed it?

I can't remember how, but in the end I accepted the intense sadness of seeing that man imprisoned in his resentment, yet I didn't give in to the seduction of discouragement. I entrusted him and his family to the intercession of the Blessed Virgin Mary, and I threw myself with renewed vigor into the rest of my priestly duties. Maybe I couldn't reach that man, but with God's grace maybe I would be able to reach some others.

Jesus himself sometimes experienced profound sadness. He wept over the city of Jerusalem, which refused to receive his message of salvation; he wept over the death of his friend Lazarus; and his soul became "sorrowful even to death" in the Garden of Gethsemane (Mark 14:34).

In his Sermon on the Mount, Jesus proclaimed that experiencing sadness over these kinds of things, a sadness in harmony with truth, helps us move forward on the path of a meaningful life: "Blessed are those who mourn," he taught, "for they will be comforted" (Matthew 5:4). Paul also commented on the difference between healthy and unhealthy sadness: "For godly sorrow produces a salutary repentance without regret, but worldly sorrow produces death" (2 Corinthians 7:10).

Simple sadness recognizes and accepts the damage that sin and evil bring into the world. But it doesn't stop there. The love and humility that allow us to feel the pain of loss and injustice also open the door to hope. God has revealed that even though the crucifixion is real, so is the resurrection. Good Friday eventually yielded to Easter. Just so, healthy sadness makes us feel the goodness of life more poignantly and moves us to invest our time and energy in things that will truly matter, things that will last forever and shine under the brilliant light of eternal life.

We don't need to be afraid of feeling sad. But we do need to be afraid of caving in to discouragement. Here again we detect the wisdom of the seasons. The touch of sadness that comes with autumn is sweet, because it is part of a bigger story, a story of life, and growth, and fruitfulness. Sadness is true, but not the whole truth. As Jesus promised, it is that whole truth that will lead us to lasting interior freedom: "If you remain in my word, you will truly be my disciples, and you will know the truth, and the truth will set you free" (John 8:31–32).

## Making It Your Own

† Choose one sentence from this chapter that really resonated in your heart or compose a one-sentence summary. Write it on a sticky note. Put it where you will see it throughout the week as a reminder that healthy sadness has an important role to play in our life's pilgrimage.

† Think of someone you know who is going through a period of loss and understandable sadness. Think of how you could reach out to comfort that person this week and help assure that his or her healthy sadness doesn't fester into paralyzing discouragement.

† Reflect prayerfully on the saddest moments of your past life. What truth did those experiences show you? How did you deal with the sadness that came over you? What can you learn from those experiences that can help you deal even better with future sadness?

† Reflect prayerfully on what tends to lead you beyond healthy sadness and into unhealthy discouragement. Write down these reflections in a journal to help clarify your thoughts. Try to discover patterns that can help you recognize more quickly in the future the arrival of this subtle but dangerous temptation.

† Take a walk in nature this week. Allow yourself to feel the mood of the season, to echo that mood in your own emotions. Pay attention to what you feel. Simply enjoy those feelings, accepting them and allowing them to take their proper place within the larger story of your life as seen through God's eyes.

# Chapter 8: *Friendship*

The natural world seems to breathe a sigh of relief as autumn makes its appearance. It seems to slow down a bit, to relax and become introspective. Here again we see the effect of shorter days and chillier temperatures. Summer invited long hours of hard work and late nights of spontaneous fun. Autumn shifts gears. Not that we stop working during the fall, but our rhythm changes. The pace seems steadier and, at least in terms of the natural world, slower.

This change of pace often overflows into our behavior. Instead of thinking mostly about what we want to go off and do, what fresh adventures we want to have and new projects we want to take up, we sometimes find ourselves hankering after simple things like an unrushed conversation with a friend. While the fall winds blow and the brittle leaves scrape and rustle, we find ourselves enjoying a cup of hot apple cider as we sit by the fireplace and gaze out the window.

Such precious moments often show a tinge of melancholy. And so we don't like to share them with just anyone. But we do like to share them with those special people we call friends. A friend knows how to accompany us in those reflective moments without breaking the mood. A friend shares not only our values and hopes but also our sensibilities. As friends we can sit silently or strike up a conversation with equal effortlessness and comfort. In the season of autumn, superficial and passing things seem to dissolve, leaving the substantial things more clearly in view. Friendship is like that. When the titillating and distracting flurry of acquaintanceships and fashionable social encounters ebbs, we go back to our friends to help us filter what matters from what doesn't and to find our anchor once again.

I had a teacher once who became a friend. I still remember when the teacher-student relationship began to transition into a friendship.

It was my senior year of high school, and I had just been injured in a football game. I tore the ligaments in my knee and had to have reconstructive surgery. Back then recovery from this kind of surgery took a long while. I still remember the helplessness I felt spending six weeks on crutches, and then there was the long and arduous road of rehabilitation.

I had always been active in school. I loved being involved and busy. But with my injury, that changed. I had to slow down, but none of my buddies did. I was left somewhat alone and isolated. I don't know how I would have reacted if I had had to make that transition by myself. I think I could easily have become discouraged and maybe even depressed. But as it turned out, I didn't have the chance.

As soon as I came back to school after the surgery, one of my teachers showed an interest in my recovery. He knew the dangers of discouragement and intervened to offset them. And he didn't just point me in the right direction; he accompanied me along the way.

In free periods and after school, he would arrange for me to watch some educational videos on classical music, history, or art—subjects he knew I liked. He sometimes watched them with me, pausing to explain things, to answer my questions, to stimulate reflection. He even arranged for me to go to hear a live concert of the Cleveland Orchestra, something I had never done before.

In short, this teacher reached out to me in a way that went beyond mere duty. He had no agenda except helping me get through the difficult time in a fruitful way. I sensed his sincerity and simple generosity. As a result, he became someone I went to frequently that year for advice and guidance. In those conversations, too, he showed a genuine interest and self-effacing sincerity. After I went off to college I continued to stay in touch with him, even more than with most of my high school peers. By the time I graduated from the university and began my road to the priesthood, we had truly become friends.

In a sense, I think he taught me what friendship really is. It's a mysterious connection between two people that goes deeper than changing circumstances—even though it always emerges in the midst of them. It involves a mutual recognition of each other's existential goodness and can blossom anywhere, even in the soil of natural relationships like that between a father and a son. It enables us to share our lives with another person in a way that enriches both. It includes a mutual esteem that weathers storms, even sins. It gives human life its most human touch. In a very real sense, authentic friendship is the scent of heaven.

Friendship is something meant to last forever. It is a category of human experience that God himself has explicitly praised and encouraged. The Old Testament paints a glowing picture of friendship, revealing how much God values it, and how much he wants us to value it:

> Faithful friends are a sturdy shelter;
> whoever finds one finds a treasure. Faithful
> friends are beyond price, no amount can

balance their worth. Faithful friends are life-saving medicine; those who fear God will find them. Those who fear the Lord enjoy stable friendship, for as they are, so will their neighbors be (Sirach 6:14–17).

And during the Last Supper, the moment in the New Testament when Jesus establishes his new and everlasting covenant with the Church, Jesus explains that through his Incarnation, passion, death, and resurrection, he is changing the very nature of how we relate to God. God no longer wishes us simply to worship and serve him from afar; rather, he wants us to walk with him along life's journey, sharing in his life and in his wisdom as his friends:

I no longer call you slaves, because a slave does not know what his master is doing. I have called you friends, because I have told you everything I have heard from my Father (John 15:15).

Valuing friendship means, among other things, taking time to spend with our friends—and during the naturally slower season of autumn, we feel drawn to do just that. It also means *being* the kind of friend that we ourselves would like to have. Here we discover a perhaps surprising application of the Golden Rule, "Do to others as you would have them do to you" (Luke 6:31): Be to your friends the kind of friend that you wish them to be to you.

How can we do that? The easiest way is to learn from the experts, from the inventor of friendship himself, Jesus. Living close to him, getting to know him, studying his life and teaching and example, learning about those who have discovered and lived in his friendship (the saints)—this is a sure way to keep this essential ingredient active so that we can live deeply and richly amid the often superficial hustle and bustle of the seductive postmodern fashions swirling all around us. As one spiritual writer put it not too long ago:

> An "adult" faith is not a faith that follows the trends of fashion and the latest novelty; a mature adult faith is deeply rooted in friendship with Christ. It is this friendship that opens us up to all that is good and gives us a criterion by which to distinguish the true from the false, and deceit from truth….Our redemption is brought about in this communion of wills: being friends of Jesus, to become friends of God. The more we love Jesus, the more we know him, the more our true freedom develops and our joy in being redeemed flourishes. Thank you, Jesus, for your friendship! (*Homily Pro Eligendo Romano Pontifice*)

## Making It Your Own

† Choose one sentence from this chapter that really resonated in your heart or compose a one-sentence summary. Write it on a sticky note. Put it where you will see it throughout the week as a reminder of the beauty and importance of authentic friendship.

† Make a visit to a church or a chapel this week, and in the presence of the Lord remember and thank him for all the friends who have helped give your life sweetness, depth, direction, and joy.

† Take time this week to reflect prayerfully on what kind of a friend you have been throughout the past year. How faithful and dependable have you been? How reasonable have your efforts to invest in the friendships that are important for you in this season of your life been? What would you like to change in how you are living out your friendships? What steps will you take to do so? Write down your thoughts in a journal to help them come into focus.

† How would you describe your relationship with God? How well does the word *friendship* describe it? What would have to change to make your relationship with God more—or

deeper—of a friendship? Identify one concrete action you can perform this week that moves you in that direction. Write it in your calendar to help you remember it.

† Think of an old friend you haven't had contact with for a long time, regardless of the reason. Reach out to that person this week, if only to say thank you and share a fond memory or two. Pay attention to how doing this makes you feel and reflect prayerfully on why it makes you feel that way.

# Chapter 9: *Sacredness*

When the harvest is gathered and the ebullient life of summer has thoroughly retreated, the world around us gives us a glimpse of another world, one we cannot see directly with our physical eyes. It is this way with all the seasons, in a certain sense, but more so perhaps with autumn, because autumn is a time of collecting fruits.

Fruits don't come from the grocery store. They come from the earth, the sunlight, the wind, and the rain. They grow and mature through various seasons under an impulse of life that we discover and cultivate but whose origin and mysterious influence reach far beyond our limited powers of perception and manipulation.

It is no coincidence that the gradual development of agriculture went hand in hand with a revolution in religion. The regular rhythms of the seasons, observed and followed through generations, led to an awareness of the rhythms of growth and fruition. Hunting and gathering was little by little supplemented with some basic planting and harvesting. Modest success in these endeavors led some nomadic peoples to settle down more permanently. Stable settlements allowed for more studied practice of horticulture, and peasant cultures emerged.

From these arose the first civilizations, which were all based on a concept called theogamy, the bringing together (*gamy*) of the absolute stability and predictability of the seasonal rhythms of the physical world, whose origins were clearly divine (*theos*), and the less stable rhythms of human life. The more the social order of the first cities could mimic the divine order of the stars and seasons, the more our human reality would take on divine characteristics. The bridge, then, that enabled human beings to move from the profane to the sacred was nature.

When you hear the word *sacred*, what do you think of? We often associate sacred things with religious things, which is understandable. But just as often our experience of religious things is rather mundane. Here is one of the unfortunate ironies of the human endeavor: The trappings of religion, which are supposed to be our doorway into the sacred, sometimes become just the opposite. Rituals and traditions, artwork and ceremonies can get stuffy. Instead of inspiring us with feelings of awe and wonder, they bore and tire us.

When that happens, we must resist. We must find a way to stir up our sense of awe and mystery, because that sense alone draws us toward the fulfillment of our deepest human yearnings: communion with God. Spiritual retreats and pilgrimages are activities designed to refresh our religious senses. We should make room for them. But in our fast-paced and technologically saturated modern culture, sometimes extended and intentional contact with the natural world can also jump-start our innate human capacity for awe and wonder. We just need to give it the space to do so.

My first Catholic Easter happened before I was a Catholic. It was during my junior year overseas, where I was studying in Florence, Italy. I was in Italy for Easter, and my host family invited me to join them on their usual Holy Week and Easter Week trip to a country house that had been in the family for generations. It was located in the town of Asolo, in the northeastern region of Veneto. Like so many of the Italian hill towns, Asolo had a unique charm and personality that penetrates and soothes your soul as soon as you step into its warm embrace. In Asolo's case, much of its beauty is linked to its setting, wonderfully and providentially perched on a hill among a small cluster of mountains. As such, it is known as "The City of a Hundred Horizons."

Of course, I didn't know any of that when I showed up in my tennis shoes and blue jean jacket to enjoy my host family's hospitality. Nor did I realize that the sacred days of Holy Thursday, Good Friday, and Holy Saturday were to be celebrated in accordance with ancient traditions—processions through the streets, liturgies and musical prayer services, altars of repose and richly ornamented vestments. Such trappings of religion were new to me. I found them fascinating and beautiful, but I didn't know what they were for. I wanted to be carried away by them into some sort of religious ecstasy, but although I participated in the celebrations with all the good will I could gather, I found them tiresome.

But then Easter morning arrived. I had slept on the living room floor the previous night and, before dawn, I awoke with a start. As soon as I opened my eyes I was fully, joyfully, inquisitively awake. Everyone else was still snoring. I had a strange sense that I had been awakened by an angel or by some stroke of providence at the very least. The thought popped into my head that I needed to go and see the sunrise on this Easter morning. I needed to celebrate Christ's rising from the dead by watching God orchestrate the rising of the sun. So off I went.

No one else in the town seemed to be up. The previous night's activities had gone long and the town was sleeping tranquilly and gladly. I was alone as I padded through the medieval streets and guessed what twists and turns would lead farther up the hill. All I knew was that I needed an unobstructed view of the great event, so I had to climb high enough above the nearby hilltops and mountains to see the horizon. Somehow, I found my way to the perfect place. I stood there on a small clearing atop a small mountain, and mist wafted gently up from all the valleys below me, wrapping me in a chilly but refreshing embrace. The sky was just beginning to pale in the east, and I saw where the sun was soon to appear.

I was alone, young, hearty, and surrounded by the secret beauties that belong only to sunrises, but I wasn't thinking about any of that. Something else was unfolding. I sensed it. This was not just a nature lover's jaunt in the Italian countryside. This was a moment of revelation, an invitation from the Other Side—it was *sacred*. I don't know how I knew, but I knew. And so I stood very still, heart thrilling, mind relaxed, eyes eager to behold whatever would come.

Then the sun broke over the edge of the horizon, its dazzling brightness more like liquid gold than mere light. It continued to rise, and before, beneath, and above me I watched the world transform. I watched the liquid gold pour over the landscape and impart a brilliant, fresh vitality to everything it touched, from the treetops to the tiny rooftops to the dark corners whose shadows fled before the silent, glorious advance of the rising sun, the new day, the Easter dawn.

I was transfixed, and at the same time,

transported. In this moment of grace, it felt as if I was being offered a vision of spiritual truth in the form of natural beauty. I knew, I couldn't deny it, that the offer was a gesture of love, a message from my Lord and my God, a gift to strengthen, inspire, and encourage me in the path of my sincere but youthful search for the meaning of life.

The experience of the sacred is a gift, but it seems to be a necessary gift if we want to live life to the full. One theory about the etymology of the word *religion* traces it back to the Latin term *re-ligare*, which means "to reconnect." Sin, evil, and the other wounds of this fallen world have distanced us from the intimacy with God that our hearts were made to enjoy. Religion, with its ensemble of beliefs and practices and moral norms, is meant to reconnect us to God, to be a path of redemption and reconciliation, a road to reunion with our Creator and heavenly Father.

If we never experience sacredness personally and existentially, all those beliefs and rituals can easily fall short of their goal and leave us bored, even cold. We need to pray and hope for sacred encounters to assure that doesn't happen.

Unless we truly experience sacredness, that awe-inspiring presence of the divine glancing out at us from behind the bright mystery of this passing world and thrilling the soul, we will find it difficult to grow in our relationship with

God. God is the holy one, the source of all good and beautiful things, and we are made to live in communion with him. Unless he reveals himself to us in this way and unless we are open to accept the revelation and respond to it, we never really find the path that leads to the fulfillment we yearn for.

Jesus made this clear when explaining the mystery of his kingdom. He told his followers, "No one can come to me unless the Father who sent me draw him....Everyone who listens to my Father and learns from him comes to me" (John 6:44–45). To be drawn toward the Lord by God, by a mysterious whisper in the depths of the soul that stokes the flame of eternity burning in the deepest center of who we are—this is the experience of the sacred.

Autumn is full of whispers. The noise of summer is over. The silence of winter has not yet descended. The whispers of fall, the sacred murmurs and sighs of this marvelous but aching world come to us and invite us to stop our frenetic activity, clear our minds of needless distractions, and look with childlike eyes at the wonders of the season. If we can muster up enough courage to do so, we may rediscover the sacredness that makes life worth living, and that makes all the lovely, mysterious, and symbolic expressions of religion glimmer and resonate as the bridges to God they are truly meant to be.

## Making It Your Own

† Choose one sentence from this chapter that really resonated in your heart or compose a one-sentence summary. Write it on a sticky note. Put it where you will see it throughout the week as a reminder to keep your heart and mind open for a glimpse of the sacred.

† Take time this week to reflect prayerfully over your most intense past experiences of the sacred. What prompted them? What did they feel like? What effect did they have on your life? Write down your thoughts in a journal in order to give them focus.

† Think of a friend or acquaintance whose religiosity you respect, either for its consistency, its depth, its simplicity, or its fruits. Invite that person out for a cup of coffee and ask about his or her experiences of the sacred. Ask this person to share his or her story with you. Enjoy hearing it and allow yourself to marvel at how God has worked in that person's life.

† Visit a sacred place this week—a shrine, a church, a memorial, or even a place that may only be sacred to you. Allow yourself to slow down and simply absorb the message and the feeling of that place. Pray there. Ask God for

the grace to be open to what is sacred and to live in such a way as to be worthy of the gift of more experiences of the sacred.

† Reflect prayerfully on how you are living the religious rituals in your life—from Sunday Mass to grace before meals to everything in between. How deeply are you penetrating the meaning of these gestures? Is empty routine creeping into any of them? How would you like to be living them, and what can you do this week to live at least one of them more intentionally and fruitfully?

# Chapter 10: *Balance*

They say timing is everything. The right word spoken at the wrong time becomes the wrong word. The right decision executed at the wrong moment becomes a mistake. The right road followed in the wrong moment disrupts the journey. Things have their proper times. Learning to discern them, learning to determine when to be silent and when to speak, when to act and when to wait, when to intervene and when to let things unfold—these, too, are lessons autumn teaches.

Autumn doesn't teach us how to make every choice wisely. Every choice involves a unique combination of factors, so no universal formula can apply in every situation. But autumn does teach us, or at least reminds us, of the simple fact that different circumstances often require different solutions. What brings the glory of autumn into view is a lessening of sunlight and a drop in temperature—the very opposite of what stimulates the glory of spring. When harvest time comes, we must act quickly, before the first frost works its mischief—such quickness and urgency acted upon during the summer, when patient cultivation is in order, would yield nothing but ruin and waste.

Our journey through life is in many ways like a walk on a balance beam. With each step we take, we must make some adjustment, slight or great, to keep moving forward. The balance that keeps us straight at one point along the beam will not keep us straight further on. We are not machines, but people. As such, we must learn to be flexible, to bend but not break when the wild winds blow, like the tall and noble bamboo shoots so suggestive in Asian art. Balance and equilibrium, spiritually and emotionally, give us the stability in life that we desire, but it's a dynamic stability, not a static one. We are human beings, not statues.

The year before I was ordained I had the grace and the privilege to become somewhat involved in the making of the film *The Passion of the Christ*. Through a few providential encounters, I got to know some of the people working on it as they were filming in Italy and spent time on the set. I have written a book titled *Inside the Passion* about what I believe to be the artistic and religious brilliance of the movie, which I am convinced every Christian should see. But one aspect of its production illustrates with particular eloquence the value of balance, of knowing how to adjust to different seasons and circumstances, to bend without breaking. It was how the director worked with his actors.

Mel Gibson had already received an Academy Award for Best Director in 1996 for his work on *Braveheart*, but to know that someone is a great director is quite different from seeing one in action. Spending time on the set of *The Passion* gave me a chance to do just that. What struck me most was how differently he worked with each one of his actors. With one he would have long conversations and include long pauses between takes. With another he would barely say anything at all. With yet another he would demonstrate with his own face and voice what he was looking for, and with others he would give sharp and clear instructions. It was almost as if there were a dozen different directors working on the film—he varied his direction style that much.

And it worked. He was able to help all the actors put forth their best performances. It wasn't through some kind of mechanical formula. It wasn't through imposing the same method on each one. Rather, it was through a keen sensitivity to the needs and talents of each, through his ability to adjust and react deftly and creatively to each personality and scene. The results spoke for themselves, as the movie, although it was filmed in Latin and Aramaic and everyone already knew the plot, became the most successful R-Rated production in Hollywood history, by far. It is still watched by millions every year as Easter draws near.

Knowing how to adapt was a key element in the creative process of making that movie, and it is also a key element in the creative process of life. People go through seasons, situations change, and what is right and proper in one moment may need some tweaking a little later. We need to be aware of this and learn to live with balance.

One of my favorite passages from the Bible presents this uncomfortable and perplexing truth as a series of contrasts:

> There is an appointed time for everything,
> and a time for every affair under the heavens.
>
> A time to give birth, and a time to die;
> a time to plant, and a time to uproot the plant.
>
> A time to kill, and a time to heal;
> a time to tear down, and a time to build.
>
> A time to weep, and a time to laugh;
> a time to mourn, and a time to dance.
>
> A time to scatter stones, and a time to
> gather them;
> a time to embrace, and a time to be far
> from embraces.

A time to seek, and a time to lose;
a time to keep, and a time to cast away.

A time to rend, and a time to sew;
a time to be silent, and a time to speak.

A time to love, and a time to hate;
a time of war, and a time of peace.

*Ecclesiastes 3:1–8*

In our technologically programmed post-modern culture, these kinds of statements don't make sense. It's hard for us to appreciate the dynamic equilibrium of life, with its seasons that appear so contradictory and yet are so mutually beneficial— even necessary. We have formed habits of mind that make us tend to see things mechanically, not vitally. We want perfect clarity, perfect formulas. We flee the complexities and mysterious unpredictability of life. We fear the very flexibility that will allow us to live each moment to the full.

But in order to live the balance, we need a center of gravity. What is it? According to Jesus, it is *the truth*—the truth he spoke to us about God's existence, the truth about the purpose of our lives as God has revealed it, the truth about moral goodness, the truth about the profound meaning that our Lord has given even to our sufferings.

The truth that is summed up in the sign of Christ's cross is the center of gravity that enables us to find our balance and live in authentic freedom no matter what. To again quote one of Jesus' most memorable sayings: "If you remain in my word, you will truly be my disciples, and you will know the truth, and the truth will set you free" (John 8:31–32).

If we keep seeking Christ's truth and live in it when we find it, our lives will have both stability and flexibility, and we will experience, more and more, the "glorious freedom of the children of God" (Romans 8:21). From this perspective, our Lord's advice in his Sermon on the Mount becomes very practical: "But seek first the kingdom [of God] and his righteousness, and all these things will be given you besides" (Matthew 6:33).

To keep our balance, then, all we need to do is to keep our hand in Jesus' hand, the hand that made us, and the only hand that can steadily guide us to the more abundant life we long for.

## Making It Your Own

† Choose one sentence from this chapter that really resonated in your heart or compose a one-sentence summary. Write it on a sticky note. Put it where you will see it throughout the week as a reminder that "there is an appointed time for everything, and a time for every affair under the heavens."

† What types of experiences tend to knock you off balance, leading you to say or do things you later regret? Reflect on your past experience to identify those patterns and then put a name on the influences that throw you for a loop. Reflect prayerfully on what God has to say to you about those things. Write down your conclusions in a journal to give them focus and clarity.

† Take time this week to reflect prayerfully on the rhythm of your life—think about it in terms of daily, weekly, monthly and yearly rhythms. What elements, if any, have become too mechanical and rigid? What elements demonstrate the wisdom of the seasons and exhibit a healthy balance and flexibility? What elements have become so flexible that they have lost their integrity? Think about one or two things that you would like to change in

light of this reflection. Write down concrete actions you can take this week to move toward those changes.

† What typically makes you lose your temper? Why? What can you do to change that behavior pattern in the future?

† Visit a notable bridge in your area this week. Maybe read about its construction and special characteristics before visiting it. During your visit, contemplate the combination of contrasting elements that gives the bridge its strength, beauty, and functionality. Try to identify where realities like balance, equilibrium, and tension between contrasts come together to contribute to those elements. Write down in a journal the lessons from this contemplation that you feel apply to your own life.

# Chapter 11: *Wisdom*

Every season has its own peculiar type of wisdom. Autumn's wisdom has to do with planning ahead. To survive the coming winter, the fall harvest must be gathered on time and properly stored. The fruit is transformed into preserves, the seed corn is piled high in the silos, and the wood is chopped, stacked, and made ready for the long, cold months ahead. It is work of preparation that requires thinking long term. Learning from experience, knowing what's coming (at least in general terms), and making the necessary sacrifices now to be able to manage well later are all part of this brand of autumn wisdom.

Of course, the prudent planner differs greatly from the control freak. The wise know that even the best plans may have to be changed, because so many factors are beyond direct human influence. As the Book of Proverbs puts it: "Many are the plans of the human heart, but it is the decision of the Lord that prevails" (Proverbs 19:21). Yet the simple reality that we are not in control of every circumstance and eventuality doesn't contradict the wisdom of planning ahead; it only tempers and shapes it. As the same Book of Proverbs says about hard work in summer and prudent planning at harvest time:

> Go to the ant, O sluggard, study her ways and learn wisdom; For though she has no chief, no commander or ruler, she procures her food in the summer, stores up her provisions in the harvest (Proverbs 6:6–8).

The rhythms that God has built into the world require us to enjoy the present moment without forgetting that it will pass and tomorrow will come with its own challenges and opportunities. We should always be ready.

Being a control freak is one way to shed autumn wisdom, but it isn't the only way. Another strain of our post-modern culture invites us to abandon all thought of the future and cling desperately to the present moment, as if it existed in a vacuum. This is the extreme of hedonism, of irresponsibility and perpetual adolescence. It, too, contains a grain of truth—we *are* supposed to live the present moment to the full—but it distorts that truth and inflates it way out of proportion, flattening the multiple dimensions of the human spirit to the single plane of present pleasure. The wisdom of autumn, the wisdom that appreciates the here-and-now without idolizing it, is an antidote for this exaggeration, too.

Through the ages, many spiritual writers have

applied this wisdom to the process of growing in spiritual maturity. They point out that holiness is the result of a partnership. On the one hand, God himself must supply the grace, just as he supplies existence itself, with all the laws of physics and biology that give order and consistency to the universe. On the other hand, some people achieve holiness and others don't, which implies that God won't do all the work himself. God asks us to participate, to do our part. Just as the farmer doesn't give his plants their power to grow, but he harvests them, stores their fruits, and rations them to last out the winter.

During my sophomore year of college I received a research fellowship from the National Endowment for the Humanities. As a result, I spent the summer months commuting between my university and a small town in central California called Mokelumne Hill. The idea was to investigate the founding and development of the town during the nineteenth century westward-expansion period in light of the social contract theories of the Enlightenment thinker John Locke. I was fascinated by Locke's philosophy, but I had my suspicions as to how well his philosophical affirmations about the origins of human society reflected the nitty-gritty reality of actual social development. So I dug into the archives of the town to compare theories with actualities.

My commute required me to drive through the beautiful foothills in that part of California, and I often stopped to take in the view. One day I parked the car high up in the foothills and ate my lunch sitting near the edge of a cliff. It was a lovely, hazy California summer day, and I luxuriated in the heat and the gorgeous view. As I gazed, I looked down into the valley below. I glimpsed a bird circling lazily—so far down that it was just a speck. It caught my attention and I kept watching it. Gradually, I realized that it was rising. Its huge wingspan was fully extended, and it seemed to be rising on the air currents. As it rose closer to my altitude, I saw that it was an eagle, noble, beautiful, and mesmerizing. I kept watching. And then I realized something. As long as this bird had been in view, its wings had been spread, but it had never flapped them. I wondered how long it could remain in flight and on course without moving its wings. So I kept watching, lunch completely forgotten.

The minutes passed, and it reached my level on the mountainside. It continued circling, rising, and simply riding the air currents with its wings spread wide. I was transfixed. It rose and rose, until once again it was only a speck, but this time a speck far above me.

Never once did I see that eagle flap its wings, but neither did I see it retract them. In that very moment the thought popped into my head that this is how God wanted me to live. He wanted me to spread my wings, to have no fear and do my part, but it would be his grace, his loving breath, that would allow me to rise to fulfillment. The sight was a living parable, an invitation to work hard in life, but always peacefully, always joyfully, always confident that in the end it would be God who made it all worthwhile.

Jesus spoke often about the future, but in spiritual terms, not just in terms of preparing for winter after the autumn harvest. He never wanted us to become obsessed with trying to create heaven on earth: "Do not fret over tomorrow," he warned us, "let tomorrow fret over its own cares; for today, today's troubles are enough" (Matthew 6:34, *Knox* translation). Yet he never tired of pointing out that this earthly life is just a preparation for what is to come, and how we use the time allotted us here will have a proportionate impact on what we experience for all eternity. In his unforgettable parable of the talents, for instance, he draws a clear parallel between our earthly behavior and our heavenly reward:

> His master said to him, "Well done, my good and faithful servant. Since you were faithful in small matters, I will give you great responsibilities. Come, share your master's joy" (Matthew 25:23).

It's just one of many examples that could be given. Jesus made it clear that we're to keep the afterlife in mind while we endeavor to live life well here and now, just as we are to keep winter in mind as we enjoy the fall harvest. Saint Paul echoed this idea. Though he often instructs that salvation comes to us as a gift of grace accepted through faith, he also reminds us that God:

> …will repay everyone according to his works: eternal life to those who seek glory, honor, and immortality through perseverance in good works, but wrath and fury to those who selfishly disobey the truth and obey wickedness. Yes, affliction and distress will come upon every human being who does evil…But there will be glory, honor, and peace for everyone who does good (Romans 2:6–10).

How we decide to live today will have repercussions tomorrow, just as what we do with our time in the fall will affect how we get along in the winter. This is the seasonal wisdom of autumn, revealed by our Lord as a whisper of eternal wisdom, as an invitation to enjoy the present moment properly, but always with an eye to its fulfillment in eternity.

Autumn is intimately connected to summer, as to its source and fullness. But it is also intimately connected to winter, as dusk is to night. Have we allowed the post-modern obsession with thinking only of the current pleasure to obscure this prudent perspective from our daily decisions and activities? If so, no time is better than now to reclaim this wisdom, which is part of our heritage as people called to begin our journey to eternity from within the beautiful and mysterious dimensions of time and space.

## Making It Your Own

† Choose one sentence from this chapter that really resonated in your heart or compose a one-sentence summary. Write it on a sticky note. Put it where you will see it throughout the week as a reminder of the lessons that autumn wisdom wants to teach us.

† Do you tend to obsess about planning out every detail of your life, or do you tend to prefer spontaneity and impulsiveness to a fault? Take time to prayerfully reflect on which tendency is more present in your life and why. Write down your reflections and then make a concrete resolution to help you implement the wisdom of autumn in a proactive way.

† Think of a famous person who has always intrigued you—a saint, perhaps, or someone who made a contribution to society that you have long admired. Find a good biography about that person and commit to reading it. As you do, pay attention to how that person balanced a healthy prudence about the future with a healthy freedom in the present.

† Take time this week to calmly look forward to the year ahead. List the commitments you already have and think about some goals you would like to achieve—maybe even some new habits you would like to form or some bad habits you would like to get rid of. In light of the insights that come up during this time of reflection, make some reasonable plans about your future.

† The only mammal that walks upright, face forward, is the human being. Through the centuries, philosophers have observed that this reflects the unique human capacity for abstract thought, for thinking ahead, and making a lasting impact on the world. When have you experienced the positive results of planning ahead? When have you experienced the negative results that can come from irresponsibly not planning ahead? Reflect prayerfully on those experiences and write down in a journal the lessons that come to you.

# Chapter 12: *Detachment*

If we are honest, we have to admit that the gradually fading glory of autumn is also a gentle hint of death. Fall is the sunset of summer. When the fields are harvested and the fruit trees are picked, when the golden leaves turn brown and brittle and are swept into nature's corners by the crisp fall breezes, and when the broad and brooding harvest moon has had its boastful say, little remains of the lush summer green or the bright spring blooms. Death has deftly and smugly plied its sickle once again.

Somehow, though, the death of autumn has a sweetness to it. Its melancholy mood attracts, instead of repels. It draws us toward it. It invites us to walk with it and listen to its silent plea. Under the guise of autumn, death shows itself to be a natural companion, or, as St. Francis of Assisi famously dubbed it, our sister. Yes, things pass, death comes and steals them away, and yet we know that such is the way of this earth. Our grief is blunted by this knowledge, by this yearly tour of brown grass, bare limbs, raked lawns, and fallow fields. Here in our fallen world, death, though often unwelcome, is not a stranger. Death teaches us detachment, the hard but necessary lesson that we should not cling too strongly to anything here below, because everything earthly fades away. As the medieval monks used to put it, *sic transit gloria mundi,* thus passes the glory of this passing world.

My first full-time job was working in a cemetery. I took a summer job working for the street department in my hometown, and I was assigned to the Evergreen Cemetery crew. We started each morning at 6 AM and finished at 3 PM. We spent the day cutting grass, trimming bushes and trees, installing headstones, cleaning up after funerals, and doing all the other labor associated with keeping a graveyard up to snuff.

At first I was anxious about it. I thought it would be spooky working there. But very quickly I realized that it wasn't, at least not for any of the veterans. For the sexton and the other experienced workers, the cemetery seemed to have lost almost all its otherworldly aura. I detected, I think, a latent respect for the place, but it was buried, so to speak, beneath a thick veneer of routine and monotony. This perplexed me. I was especially confounded—at least at first—by the typical reaction when a burial was scheduled to take place. We had to shut down all the machinery and wait for the ceremony to finish before returning to work, so we usually sat in the sexton's shed and played cards while the mourners gathered and paid their last respects to their dead relative or friend. It seemed hardhearted to me, and I couldn't bring myself to join the games, which earned me plenty of sarcastic jibes.

Even so, I remained keenly aware throughout the entire summer of the sacredness of the place. I believe now that this awareness was a grace from God. I was no stranger to death, since my mother had passed away when I was only nine years old. But I had little religious formation at the time, so I had never really thought about death in a serious way. But that summer I did. I worked hard, but I also found time to read the tombstones, to explore the different sections of the cemetery, to notice that some graves were from as far back as the Civil War, and some marked the burial places of octogenarians, while others marked the tiny resting places of infants.

The reality of death, of the impermanence of things, of the unpredictability of what we prized most highly and took for granted most easily— life—penetrated my mind and my heart. I mulled it over and over and over. I imagined the lives that had been lived by the men, women, and children buried under the grass I was cutting. What had they valued? What had they left behind? Had they found what they were looking for?

I can't remember specifically if my personal search for the meaning of life—the search that led me eventually into the Catholic Church and opened me to receive the gift of my vocation to the priesthood—began during those hours working in Evergreen Cemetery. But I distinctly remember that by the time I stopped work to go back to school for my senior year the search was fully under way. I didn't want to live for anything that would dissolve when I died, so I had to find something worth living for that would last, but at the same time, I had a youthful zest for life that I didn't want to deny. What a conundrum!

Jesus understood how hard it is for us to appreciate the good things of this earth without getting overly attached to them. He spoke of heaven so often, so patiently, and so winsomely, referring to it as a banquet, a wedding feast, and everlasting joy. And he also warned against living for this life alone:

> Do not store up for yourselves treasures on earth, where moth and decay destroy, and thieves break in and steal. But store up treasures in heaven, where neither moth nor decay destroys, nor thieves break in and steal. For where your treasure is, there also will your heart be (Matthew 6:19–21).

This theme runs through the whole Bible the way a single musical motif can influence an entire symphony. Earthly life, with its intense joys and piercing beauties, is a gift from God, but it is only a place of pilgrimage, not our final destiny: "For here we have no lasting city, but we seek the one that is to come" (Hebrews 13:14). The gifts God sends us, which we are called and invited to enjoy and use in accordance with their proper purposes, are but signs of his goodness, road signs pointing to heaven. We are to love them sincerely and yet remain detached from them so that we stay free to embrace the giver himself, who is so much more than those gifts. As usual, the Psalms elucidate this truth with haunting eloquence:

> Before the mountains were born,
>> the earth and the world brought forth,
>> from eternity to eternity you are God.
>
> You turn humanity back into dust,
>> saying, "Return, you children of Adam!"
>
> A thousand years in your eyes
>> are merely a day gone by,
>
> Before a watch passes in the night,
>> you wash them away;
>
> They sleep, and in the morning they sprout
>> again like an herb.
>
> In the morning it blooms only to pass away;
>> in the evening it is wilted and withered.

*Psalm 90:2–6*

One of the most famous phrases in the entire Catholic liturgy comes from a preface used during the Holy Mass celebrated in memory of the dearly beloved who have died. It describes death, in light of Christ's own crucifixion and resurrection, as life that has "changed not ended," and in so doing it reiterates the wisdom of Christian detachment:

> In him the hope of blessed resurrection
>   has dawned,
> that those saddened by the certainty
>   of dying
> might be consoled by the promise
>   of immortality to come.
>
> Indeed for your faithful, Lord,
> life is changed not ended,
> and, when this earthly dwelling turns to dust,
> an eternal dwelling is made ready for them
>   in heaven.

*The Roman Missal, Preface I for the Dead*

In the subdued sunlight of autumn, infusing the burgundy and golden brown tones of fall with the warmth of a smiling sadness, let us take the hand of our sister, Death, in whatever way she shows herself, and trust that she, too, under the irresistible wisdom of Providence, is but one more mysterious manifestation, perhaps even a beckoning invitation, of God's eternal love.

## Making It Your Own

† Choose one sentence from this chapter that really resonated in your heart or compose a one-sentence summary. Write it on a sticky note. Put it where you will see it throughout the week as a reminder that detachment keeps us free to live life to the full.

† It is an ancient Catholic tradition to visit a cemetery on November 2, the Day of the Dead, in order to pray for the souls who have passed on and may still be undergoing purification before their entrance into heaven. It is also a way to remind ourselves that here we have no lasting city. This week, visit a cemetery and walk prayerfully among the memorials of the dead, asking God to enlighten you with the wisdom that comes from an eternal perspective.

† Each year on November 1, Catholics celebrate All Saints' Day, a day on which we commemorate all the dearly departed who are now enjoying the delights of heaven with the Lord. The revived pagan celebration of Halloween actually takes its current name from the ancient phrase "All Hallow's Eve," which means the evening before All Saints' Day. Take time this week to reflect prayerfully on heaven.

What do you think of when you think of heaven? What impact does this reality that Jesus has revealed to us have on your daily life? What impact would you like it to have?

† Take time this week to read slowly and prayerfully chapter 25 in the Gospel of St. Matthew. In this chapter Jesus teaches us about the Final Judgment and the end of history. As you read, ask the Lord to speak to your heart. Then write down in a journal what strikes you most, and try to make a concrete resolution that will help you apply one of those insights to your life this week.

† Take time this week to reflect prayerfully on what you are attached to. Think, for example, about what you would miss most if you were suddenly stranded alone on a desert island, or how you would spend ten million dollars if you won the lottery tomorrow. What do you really need to make you completely happy? Write down in a journal your reflections, to clarify them and give them focus. Decide what you will adjust in your life to live the gospel value of healthy detachment more authentically.

## About the Author

**Fr. John Bartunek, LC, ST͟HD**, a graduate of Stanford University in 1990, comes from an evangelical Christian background and became a member of the Catholic Church in 1991. He was ordained a Catholic priest in 2003 and earned his doctorate in moral theology in 2010. He is the author of *The Better Part* and *Inside the Passion: An Insider's Look at the Passion of the Christ*. Fr. Bartunek splits his time between Michigan, where he continues his writing apostolate and assists at Our Lady Queen of the Family Retreat Center in Oxford, and Rome, where he teaches theology at the Pontifical Athenaeum Regina Apostolorum.